Group's
SERENGETI
TREK™
Where Kids are WILD about God

THE MANE EVENT

LEADER MANUAL

Group®

Loveland, Colorado
www.groupvbs.com

Group resources actually work!

This Group resource helps you focus on **"The 1 Thing™"**— a life-changing relationship with Jesus Christ. "The 1 Thing" incorporates our **R.E.A.L.** approach to ministry. It reinforces a growing friendship with Jesus, encourages long-term learning, and results in life transformation, because it's:

Relational
Learner-to-learner interaction enhances learning and builds Christian friendships.

Experiential
What learners experience through discussion and action sticks with them up to 9 times longer than what they simply hear or read.

Applicable
The aim of Christian education is to equip learners to be both hearers and doers of God's Word.

Learner-based
Learners understand and retain more when the learning process takes into consideration how they learn best.

Visit our Web sites:
www.group.com
www.groupvbs.com
www.groupoutlet.com

Thanks to our talented VBS curriculum team!
Gwyn D. Borcherding, Jessica Broderick, Jody Brolsma, Teryl Cartwright, Shelly Dillon, Enelle G. Eder, Josh Emrich, Lynne Foster, Cindy S. Hansen, Lisa Harris, Tracy K. Hindman, Alison Imbriaco, Mikal Keefer, Julie Lavender, Maura Link, Linda Marcinkowski, Katie Martinez, Pat Miller, Kari K. Monson, Barbie Murphy, Peggy Naylor, Jane Parenteau, Janis Sampson, Joani Schultz, Larry Shallenberger, Pamela Shoup, Rodney Stewart, and Bonnie Temple

Unless otherwise indicated, all Scripture quotations are taken from the *Holy Bible*, New Living Translation, copyright © 1996. Used by permission of Tyndale House Publishers, Inc., Wheaton, Illinois 60189. All rights reserved. (Day 4 Treasure Verse is from the New Century Version.)

ISBN 0-7644-2789-X
Printed in the United States of America.
10 9 8 7 6 5 4 3 2 1   07 06 05

CONTENTS

THE MANE EVENT

Welcome to Serengeti Trek! 5

Your Role at Serengeti Trek 7

Serengeti Trek Overview 10

Serengeti Trek Is
Crawling With New Friends! 12

What to Expect at Serengeti Trek 13

What's the Daily Challenge™? 14

Before the Trek Begins 16

DAY 1 (Know God.) 19

DAY 2 (Talk to God.) 27

DAY 3 (Tell about God.) 33

DAY 4 (Love God.) 37

DAY 5 (Work for God.) 41

WELCOME TO SERENGETI TREK!

A giraffe casually nibbles leaves from a lush acacia tree.

A lion crouches in the tall grass, watching a herd of zebras.

Suddenly an elephant thunders by in a cloud of dust.

And you? You're standing on the vast savanna, gearing up for the adventure of a lifetime on a Serengeti Trek—where kids are wild about God!

Serengeti Trek is teeming with fun for kids, teenagers, and adults. Everyone involved in *this* VBS will pounce into God's Word...and will never be the same again! As kids explore amazing Bible adventures, they'll take part in Daily Challenges that encourage them to apply Bible truths to everyday life.

If you haven't used Group's VBS materials before, you're in for a real treat. Serengeti Trek is an exciting, fun-filled, Bible-based program your kids will love. (We know because we tested everything in a field test last summer. Look for the "Hints From the Herd" to learn how our discoveries will make *your* program the best!)

Kids start each day by forming small groups called Safari Crews. All the Safari Crews gather at Sing & Play Roar to sing and do fun motions to upbeat Bible songs that introduce kids to the concepts they'll be learning that day. Then Safari Crews visit five different Serengeti Stations. They go on wild Bible Expeditions, meet Chadder Chipmunk™ on video, make delightful Critter Crafts, play Wild Games, and sample tasty treats at Watering Hole Snacks! Then everyone comes together for the closing, The Mane Event.

LEADING THE MANE EVENT IS EASY AND FUN!

HINTS FROM THE HERD

Don't skip these fun, audience-involving, memorable programs! Although you might be tempted to simply gather kids for a few minutes of singing to wrap up each day at Serengeti Trek, skipping The Mane Event would rob kids of important learning experiences. The kids at our field test looked forward to The Mane Event each day because each program was an exciting surprise! Remember, kids learn in many different ways. This may be the glue that holds God's Word to the heart of a certain child at your VBS!

You'll enjoy your role and be most successful as the Mane Event Leader if you

- enjoy being in front of people,

- are a bit of a ham,

- like to laugh and have a good sense of humor,

- encourage and affirm kids' participation in The Mane Event each day, and

- model God's love in everything you say and do.

HINTS FROM THE HERD

We had the same person lead Sing & Play Roar and The Mane Event. Since both stations can benefit from someone who is comfortable in front of kids and doesn't mind hamming it up, we found a "natural" who could lead both.

YOUR ROLE AT SERENGETI TREK

Here's what's expected of you before, during, and after Group's Serengeti Trek.

BEFORE SERENGETI TREK

- Attend scheduled leader training.
- Pray for the kids who will attend your church's Serengeti Trek.
- Plan your wardrobe. Ask your Serengeti Trek Director (otherwise known as your church's VBS director) what you should wear to Serengeti Trek. Adult staff T-shirts (available from Group Publishing or your local Christian bookstore) will help kids identify you and help you identify other station leaders. Or you might consider wearing a khaki vest and shorts for a safari look!
- Read The Mane Event Leader Manual.
- Consult with other station leaders to recruit helpers for each day's show. You'll need at least one other person each day to help you manage props, sound, and lighting. A few jobs should be rehearsed ahead of time, but most can be completed by anyone who's available. Since preschool children need close adult supervision, don't plan on enlisting the Lion Cub Club Director unless absolutely necessary.
- Set up and check all equipment to make sure it's working properly.
- Practice each day's program three times:

  - once at home by yourself,
  - once at home in front of an honest audience (or a mirror), and
  - once in your designated station with all the equipment up and running.

DURING SERENGETI TREK

- Build enthusiasm for The Mane Event by interacting with kids throughout the day. Enjoy Watering Hole Snacks with the kids, or visit other stations to get a feel for what the kids are experiencing.
- To help create a fun atmosphere and reinforce Bible learning, play the *Sing & Play Roar Music* CD or audiocassette as kids enter and leave the room.
- Cue the *Sing & Play Roar Music* CD to the first song you'll sing during The Mane Event each day.
- Start The Mane Event on time each day.
- Have fun as you lead kids through The Mane Event activities. Be sure to smile a lot!
- Be flexible. You may need to adapt The Mane Event material to fit your facility or to accommodate a longer or shorter time frame.
- Allow a few minutes for announcements at the beginning of The Mane Event each day.

TREK TIPS

It may be helpful to meet with the Serengeti Trek Director and go over the supply list. Let the director know what supplies you have or can collect on your own and what supplies you'll need to purchase or collect from church members. Open communication makes your job even easier!

TREK TIPS

You'll find it's refreshing and relaxing not to have the busyness and pressure of a "performance." If you want parents to get a peek at Serengeti Trek, invite them to each day's closing program. (Check the Serengeti Trek Director Manual for a "Best of Serengeti Trek" open-house program, too.) Or consider doing the "Serengeti Eddy" closing production. See your Serengeti Trek catalog for information.

TREK TIPS

Kids in each Safari Crew have special jobs each day. Crew members can choose to be a Reader, Coach, Serengeti Guide, Prayer Person, or Materials Manager. Crew jobs give kids responsibilities and ensure that everyone participates in meaningful ways each day.

TREK TIPS

Tell kids to invite their parents, grandparents, or baby sitters to come to watch The Mane Event every day. Adults will want to join the celebration before they take the kids home.

TREK TIPS

The Serengeti Trek Follow-Up Kit is a great way to bring kids back to church after VBS is over. Check with your Serengeti Trek Director to see when he or she is planning this exciting (and easy!) reunion. It's a party that's just crawling with fun!

• Repeat the daily Bible Point often, and say it just as it's written. Repeating the Bible Point often, and using exactly the same words every time, will help children remember it and apply it to their lives. Kids will be listening for the day's Bible Point so they can respond by

"Wow!"

shouting "Wow!" Have kids place their fists by their mouths and then fling their fingers wide open as they shout "Wow!" The Mane Event Leader Manual suggests ways to include the Bible Point.

• Just before dismissing kids, allow two minutes for crews to take out their Daily Challenge™ papers. Crew leaders will remind kids of the Daily Challenges they've chosen, then each child will fold the Daily Challenge in half lengthwise, wrap it around his or her wrist, and fasten it in place with a Serengeti Trek sticker. For more information about the Daily Challenge, see page 14.

• *Bonus Idea!* As the Mane Event Leader, you can double as photographer (or videographer). Early in the week, follow the action with a camera loaded with slide film or with a video camera. Capture the fun kids have playing games, experiencing the Bible stories, making their crafts, and enjoying Watering Hole Snacks.

You may also want to take posed photographs of individuals and Safari Crews. Watering Hole Snacks is a great time to line kids up for these photos. At the end of the week, give the photos away to participating families as an outreach and follow-up tool. Or sell the photos to raise money for Operation Kid-to-Kid™ or to offset the costs of your VBS. You might even make double prints of crew snapshots, putting one inside each Operation Kid-to-Kid school supply kit! Kids and parents will treasure special Serengeti Trek souvenirs as reminders of an experience they'll want to hold on to for a lifetime.

Bring Bible Truths to Everyday Life!

We know that you want kids to apply Bible truths to daily life. That's why each lesson is filled with life-application activities and questions. To help you spot these important activities, just look for the Life Application logo throughout your leader manual.

AFTER SERENGETI TREK

- Return equipment to its proper place.
- Throughout the year, you can help God's love grow by
  - phoning neighborhood kids who participated in your Serengeti Trek program,
  - sending Serengeti Trek follow-up postcards, and
  - repeating segments of The Mane Event in your Sunday school or midweek programs.

SERENGETI TREK OVERVIEW

Here's what everyone else is doing! At Serengeti Trek the daily Bible Point is carefully integrated into each station activity to reinforce Bible learning. The Mane Event activities wrap up and reinforce kids' overall learning experience.

	Bible Point	Bible Story	Treasure Verse	Sing & Play Roar	Bible Expedition	Wild Games
DAY 1	Know God.	Gideon defeats the Midianites (Judges 7:1-22).	"I know the greatness of the Lord" (Psalm 135:5).	• Hear the Bible story of Gideon defeating the Midianites. • Meet Zach the Zebra Bible Memory Buddy. • Choose Safari Crew jobs. • Learn: "He's the King" "My Jesus, He Loves Me" "I Want to Know You (In the Secret)" "To God Be the Glory"	• Become part of Gideon's army. • Light a torch and know that God will help Gideon. • Tell about someone they know and trust.	**Play:** • That Face Rings a Bell • Gideon's Army Tag • "Rocka" My Soul
DAY 2	Talk to God.	Daniel prays and is sent to the den of lions (Daniel 6:1-28).	"Pray at all times" (Ephesians 6:18).	• Hear the Bible story about Daniel praying and being sent to the den of lions. • Meet Roary the Lion Bible Memory Buddy. • Learn: "Lovely Noise" "Must Be Done in Love" "Let Us Pray"	• Listen to the lions roar as they hear the story of Daniel. • Discover that Daniel prayed no matter what and that we can talk to God too. • Use a Prayer Pal to talk to God.	**Play:** • Getting Connected • Daniel in the Den • Stretch Yourself
DAY 3	Tell about God.	Shadrach, Meshach, and Abednego stand up for God (Daniel 3:1-30).	"I will tell of all the marvelous things you have done" (Psalm 9:1b).	• Hear the Bible story about Shadrach, Meshach, and Abednego standing up for God. • Meet Elaine the Crane Bible Memory Buddy. • Learn: "Famous One" "Use Me"	• Experience the Bible story of the three friends. • See a hot experiment, and decide if they would stand up for God. • Tell about modern-day idols.	**Play:** • Seen but Not "Herd" • Trek Traveling • Marvelous Madhouse
DAY 4	Love God.	Jesus dies and rises again (John 19:1–20:18).	"We love because God first loved us" (1 John 4:19).	• Hear the Bible story about Jesus dying and rising again. • Meet Gigi the Giraffe Bible Memory Buddy. • Learn: "More Love, More Power"	• Visit the garden and investigate the empty tomb. • Hear Jesus call Mary's name. • Find "evidence" to prove Jesus' resurrection.	**Play:** • Wet Sponge Juggle • Catch Me! • Wild About What?
DAY 5	Work for God.	Paul and Silas worship God in prison (Acts 16:16-40).	Work hard and cheerfully as though for the Lord (adapted from Colossians 3:23).	• Hear the Bible story about Paul and Silas worshipping God in prison. • Meet Lug the Elephant Bible Memory Buddy. • Review Sing & Play Roar songs.	• Become prisoners in a Bible-times jail. • Sing and praise God in jail.	**Play:** • Sweet 'n' Sour Smiles • Serengeti Saucers • Work-for-God Tag

This chart shows you the entire program at a glance. Refer to the chart to see how your station activities supplement other activities and help God's love grow.

Watering Hole Snacks	Chadder's Adventure Theater	Critter Crafts	The Mane Event
Gideon's Trail Mix	Chadder chooses to travel with a safari guide he knows, but now sneaky Dr. Gallstone is after them. Will Chadder and his friends accomplish their important mission?	• Bible Buddy Drum	• Review the Treasure Verse (Psalm 135:5) from the Bible. • Watch a younger child "take on" two big guys in a seemingly impossible experiment. • Sing songs to celebrate their great God. ♥ • Take home Daily Challenge reminders to show others they know God.
Daniel's Lions	Chadder and his friends spend the night surrounded by a pack of hungry lions! It's time to talk to God.	• Wild-About-Prayer Beads • Talk Talk Drum	• Watch a game show and vote for the "real" Daniel. • Review the Treasure Verse (Ephesians 6:18). • Celebrate that they can talk to God through praying and singing. ♥ • Take home Daily Challenge reminders to show others they can talk to God.
Meshach Snacks	Jabari tells Chadder about all the marvelous things God has created. But meeting a giant snake isn't so marvelous!	• African Praise Shaker • Wildlife Photo Frame	• Review the Treasure Verse (Psalm 9:1b). • Make flames in a fiery furnace and discover that they can tell about God, even when it's hard. ♥ • Take home Daily Challenge reminders to tell others about God.
Lovable Giraffes	Chadder wants to accomplish his mission to show how much he loves God. But Dr. Gallstone steals the medicine from the truck. What will happen to the sick children?	• Lovable Gigi • Wild Wobbler	• Understand that they can give their love to Jesus for his great gift of life forever. • Review the Treasure Verse (1 John 4:19). • Sing worshipful songs as they give Jesus their love. ♥ • Take home Daily Challenge reminders to show others they love God.
Jailhouse Treats	Chadder and Jabari work at the clinic...as if they're working for God. And Auntie Juji captures Dr. Gallstone and delivers the medicine in time!	• Lug's Water Blaster • Bible Memory Fun Face	• Remember what they've learned at Serengeti Trek. • Review the Treasure Verse (Colossians 3:23). ♥ • Present their Operation Kid-to-Kid™ school supply kits as an offering to God. ♥ • Take home their Daily Challenge reminders to show others they work for God.

SERENGETI TREK IS CRAWLING WITH NEW FRIENDS!

Each day at Serengeti Trek, kids meet an adorable buddy who reminds them of the day's Bible Point. They're Bible Memory Buddies®! We'll let our fun friends speak for themselves.

I'm Zach!
Zebras know other zebras by their stripe pattern. I'll remind kids to know God!

Hey, friends, it's **Elaine the Crane!**
You can tell a crowned crane is talking by its unique voice. I help kids remember to tell about God.

It's me . . . **Roary!**
Lions talk to one another really loudly! I want kids to talk to God!

My name's **Lug,**
and like all elephants, I'm a hard worker. I'll help kids remember to work hard and cheerfully for God.

To help kids remember these important Bible truths, the Chadder's Adventure Theater Leader will give each child a Bible Memory Buddy every day to keep in his or her Bible Buddy Drum (an awesome craft that kids make on Day 1). And each Buddy has the Treasure Verse inscribed on it. Kids will *love* collecting these buddies! And you'll be amazed at how the Bible Memory Buddies help kids apply Bible truths to everyday life.

Gigi here.
My long neck helps me reach the tops of trees. I want kids to love God because he reached down and loved us.

WHAT TO EXPECT AT SERENGETI TREK

If this is your first time using Group's VBS, you're in for a real treat. You're also in for some surprises! If you look beneath the surface, you'll discover that this VBS program is unlike any you've ever seen or experienced.

You might expect to see...	But at Serengeti Trek, you'll see...	That's because...
kids quietly working in workbooks.	kids talking excitedly in their Safari Crews.	crew leaders and station leaders will encourage kids to talk about important Bible truths to cement them to their lives.
a traditional school setting, with desks or tables.	kids sitting in small, knee-to-knee circles (maybe even on the floor!).	we want kids to get face to face as they talk about how to apply God's Word to their lives. (And it's just plain easier for kids to sit on the floor instead of in chairs!)
children in age-graded classrooms.	children in mixed-age groups called Safari Crews.	kids will learn so much more by interacting with children of different ages. Think of each crew as a mini-family.
classes that look neat and orderly.	lots of child-friendly movement, activity, and energy—and a little clutter, too!	we know that kids have a lot of energy—so each activity is designed to let kids actively participate in fun and exciting ways (the way God designed them!).
kids spending most of their time in one classroom.	Safari Crews traveling from station to station about every twenty minutes.	station leaders prepare only about twenty minutes of activities. Not only is that easier on leaders like you, but it keeps kids busy—so there's no time to get into trouble!
kids memorizing Bible verses to receive prizes.	kids learning—and understanding—God's Word like you've never seen before!	Bible learning should be *meaningful, delightful,* and *unforgettable.*

WHAT'S THE DAILY CHALLENGE™?

HINTS FROM THE HERD

Remember that your goal is to encourage kids to practice what they're learning just for the joy of serving Jesus! Don't offer bribes or incentives to entice kids to complete their Daily Challenges. We discovered that kids didn't need any other motivation—they were excited about choosing a Challenge and living it out!

DAILY CHALLENGE™

Of course you want kids to come to Serengeti Trek and learn about God's love. But imagine how life-changing it would be if kids took what they learned and applied it *right away* to daily life so they could "leave" God's love in the lives of others.

That's where the Daily Challenge comes in! It's as easy as 1, 2, 3!

1. During Watering Hole Snacks, kids will look over that day's Daily Challenges, found in the back of each Serengeti Trek Bible Book. Crew members will work together to choose which challenge they'll do after they leave VBS.

2. At the end of the day, The Mane Event Leader (that's you!) will have elementary kids each take that day's Daily Challenge from their Bible Books. Kids will look at the Daily Challenge again to help them remember what challenge they chose. Then each child will fold the Daily Challenge in half lengthwise and use a sticker to hold it around the wrist. Every day, each child will wear a new Daily Challenge home!

3. Before Day 2, the Sing & Play Roar Leader will place a set of acacia leaves into each Crew Bag and attach lots of Glue Dots to your acacia tree. (Leaves and Glue Dots are available at www.groupoutlet.com.) Starting on Day 2, the Sing & Play Roar Leader will ask kids who come to Sing & Play Roar to gather with their crews and talk about how they carried out their Daily Challenge. As kids share, they'll each take a leaf from the bag and hand it to the crew leader. On cue, crew leaders will come to the front and press the leaves onto the Glue Dots.

4. As the week goes on, everyone will watch as the tree comes to life. You can actually see God's love grow through children's loving actions.

What a wild way to see kids "leave" lots of God's love around all week long!

HINTS FROM THE HERD

The tree at our field test looked more like an oak tree than an acacia tree! A cool, easy-to-assemble acacia tree is available from Group Publishing or your local Christian bookstore.

BUILDING YOUR ACACIA TREE

In order to show kids that they're "leaving" lots of God's love around through the Daily Challenges, you'll need a large acacia tree at the front of your Sing & Play Roar and The Mane Event area. You can purchase this easy-to-assemble acacia tree from Group Publishing or your Group VBS supplier. Building *this* tree is as easy as 1, 2, 3!

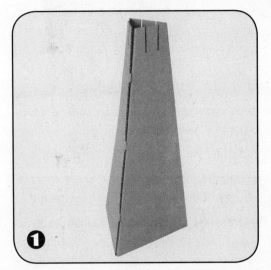

❶ Fold the trunk at the three scored lines. Fold the ends of the tabs to make them fit through the slots. Insert all three tabs into the slots, so the tabs are tucked inside the trunk.

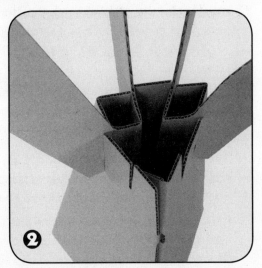

❷ Fold each section of branches in half, along the scored lines. Line up the slots on the top of the trunk with the slots on the bottom of the branch sections. (Each branch section should straddle one point of the triangular trunk.) Insert the branch section slots into the trunk slots.

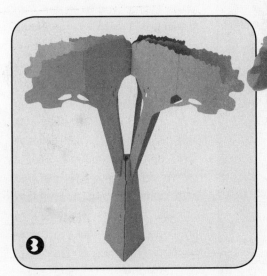

❸ Straighten the folds on all branch sections. Slip the rubber bands into the slots at the top of the tree, stretching the bands to pull the top of the tree together.

BEFORE THE TREK BEGINS

SERENGETI STATION PREPARATION

- Work with the Serengeti Trek Director to select a room for The Mane Event. You'll need a large room (such as a sanctuary or fellowship hall) that will accommodate the entire group. It's a good idea to use the same room for both The Mane Event and Sing & Play Roar.

- Remove any items that might distract children. If you're meeting in your church's sanctuary, these items might include attendance cards, hymnals, or pencils. Be sure to return all items to their proper places before your church's worship time!

- Clear the presentation area of unnecessary furniture.

- Set up (or have your church's sound technician set up) a microphone for your use. Practice with the microphone so you'll know how to turn it on and remove it from its stand.

- Set up a CD player where you'll be able to reach it easily. Or ask another station leader to assist you in turning the music on and off. If you'd like to play the CD on your church's sound system, arrange for someone to act as a sound technician for you. Be sure to agree on a signal so you'll both know when it's time to start and stop the CD. If you can't use a sound system, plan to hold a microphone to the CD player's speaker so the music will be loud enough for everyone to hear.

- If you'll be using the same area for Sing & Play Roar and The Mane Event, work with the Sing & Play Roar Leader to prepare the room. Decorate the area to look like a Serengeti grassland. Find empty refrigerator boxes and make cutouts of a child-size jeep and animals such as elephants and giraffes. Make papier-mâché rocks or termite mounds. Add a brown cloth "path." Fill the area with artificial plants and stuffed animals. Use the easy directions on page 15 to make an acacia tree. There are endless ways to transform the Mane Event area into an eye-catching, child-pleasing place!

- Photocopy the sign and arrow on pages 46-47. Make as many copies as you need to guide kids to your room.

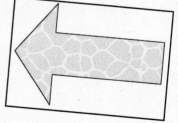

STATION SUPPLIES

DAY 1

- ❑ Bible
- ❑ CD player or sound system
- ❑ Day 1 Bible Point poster* and a paper torch (the Sing & Play Roar Leader should have these)
- ❑ Sing & Play Roar Music CD*
- ❑ 2 brooms
- ❑ 9-foot rope
- ❑ Day 1 Daily Challenge (from a Serengeti Trek Bible Book*)
- ❑ sample school supply kit
- ❑ Operation Kid-to-Kid handouts (1 handout per participant)
- ❑ tic tac drum* or other attention-getting signal

DAY 2

- ❑ Bible
- ❑ CD player
- ❑ Sing & Play Roar Music CD*
- ❑ Bible Point posters* and props for Days 1 and 2
- ❑ Day 2 Daily Challenge (from a Serengeti Trek Bible Book*)
- ❑ game show script (pp. 29-30)
- ❑ 4 volunteers (3 to be "Daniels" in the game show and 1 to be the "Applause-o-meter")
- ❑ Serengeti Trek Skits & Drama CD
- ❑ tic tac drum* or other attention-getting signal

DAY 3

- ❑ Bible
- ❑ CD player
- ❑ Sing & Play Roar Music CD*
- ❑ Bible Point posters* and props from previous days
- ❑ Day 3 Daily Challenge (from a Serengeti Trek Bible Book*)
- ❑ yellow, orange, and red streamers (enough so each person will have 2 streamers of different colors)
- ❑ tic tac drum* or other attention-getter

DAY 4

- ❑ Bible
- ❑ CD player
- ❑ Sing & Play Roar Music CD*
- ❑ Bible Point posters* and props from previous days
- ❑ Day 4 Daily Challenge (from a Serengeti Trek Bible Book*)
- ❑ "Jesus" volunteer from Bible Expedition
- ❑ large white poster board cross
- ❑ tic tac drum* or other attention-getter
- ❑ Serengeti Trek sticker sheets* or sheets of heart stickers. If using heart stickers, you'll need to put them in Crew Bags.

TREK TIPS

Attention-getting signals let kids know when it's time to stop what they're doing and look at you. You can use the tic tac drum (available from Group Publishing and your local Christian bookstore) or another noise-maker of your choice. The first time students come to your station, introduce and rehearse your attention-getting signal. Once kids are familiar with the signal, regaining their attention will become automatic.

TREK TIPS

Someone will be representing Jesus in a Bible Expedition drama on Day 4. Connect with that person ahead of time to be sure he can stay for The Mane Event.

DAY 5

❑ Bible
❑ CD player
❑ *Sing & Play Roar Music* CD*
❑ Bible Point posters* and props from previous days
❑ Day 5 Daily Challenge (from a Serengeti Trek Bible Book*)
❑ tic tac drum* or other attention-getter

*Available from Group Publishing or your local Christian bookstore.

SERENGETI TREK SAFETY TIPS

• Tape down any microphone cords so children (and you!) won't trip over them.

• To avoid accidents or lost crafts, have kids keep their crafts on the floor or in their Safari Crew Bags when they're not using them.

• If at all possible, set the action on a raised platform or stage. This will discourage children from standing on (and possibly falling off!) pews or chairs as they strain to see.

BIBLE POINT:
Know God.

BIBLE STORY:
Gideon defeats the Midianites (Judges 7:1-22).

TREASURE VERSE:
"I know the greatness of the Lord" (Psalm 135:5).

THE MANE EVENT
DAY 1

When we find Gideon in Judges 6:11, he certainly seems an unlikely hero. His people, the Israelites, have turned from God to worship idols. His land is overrun with ruthless invaders from Midian, who send the people into hiding. And Gideon? He's cowering in a wine press, threshing his wheat in secret. Is this really the man God would use to defeat an entire *army* of Midianites? It seems as if Gideon needed a reminder of who God really is.

In Judges 6, Gideon met the God his people had forgotten, and through a series of miraculous tests, God became very real to him. He discovered the power and faithfulness of a mighty God. Even as he faced a seemingly invincible army, Gideon put his complete faith in God. And because Gideon knew and trusted God, he successfully led an army of three hundred men against an enemy of thousands. Gideon's life was changed because he knew God. More important, it seems that his heart was changed.

Like the Israelites, kids today often forget the amazing things God has done in their lives. The distractions of school, friendships, sports, and clubs crowd out the importance of a life-changing relationship with God. Sometimes kids feel like the world is against them and God is nowhere to be found. The kids who come to your VBS may need to "meet" God and discover who he really is. For some kids, this will be a first-time introduction (how exciting!). For others it will be an eye-opening reminder of how awesome our God is. Use the activities in this lesson to help kids know the faithful, mighty God who loves them.

 Because I know God, I will

- discover what it means to follow God,

- explore ways to share God's love with others,

- make God part of my everyday life, and

- celebrate God.

STATION SUPPLIES

For The Mane Event today, you'll need

❏ Bible

❏ CD player or sound system

❏ Day 1 Bible Point poster and a paper torch (the Sing & Play Roar Leader should have these)

❏ *Sing & Play Roar Music* CD

❏ 2 brooms

❏ 9-foot rope

❏ Day 1 Daily Challenge (from a Serengeti Trek Bible Book)

❏ sample school supply kit

❏ Operation Kid-to-Kid handouts (1 handout per participant)

❏ tic tac drum or other attention-getting signal

TREK TIPS

Be sure the Sing & Play Roar Leader goes over the motions for the songs again, since the preschool crews won't have attended Sing & Play Roar on the first day.

HINTS FROM THE HERD

Kids of all ages loved the easy, memorable Treasure Verses! Your wiggly, kinesthetic learners will remember the words to each Treasure Verse, as they use their bodies to express the meaning.

STATION SETUP

Tie one end of a nine-foot rope to one broom handle. Wrap the rope back and forth around the broom handles. Lay the two brooms on the floor in front of the Mane Event area.

Place your Bible, Zach the Zebra poster, paper torch, and school supply kit close by. Make sure each Crew Bag has an Operation Kid-to-Kid handout for each crew member.

ONWARD TO THE EVENT!

While you're waiting for Safari Crews to arrive from their Serengeti Stations, **SAY: While we're waiting for everyone to get here, let's sing a song! When everyone hears us singing, they'll know that The Mane Event is about to begin!**

CD TRACK 1 Encourage kids to welcome the Sing & Play Roar Leader, who will lead them in singing "He's the King." Join in as everyone sings and does the motions to the song.

When everyone has arrived, **SAY: We're so glad you're here at Serengeti Trek—where kids are wild about God.** Ask kids to shout, "We're wild about God!" while they wave their hands overhead and jump up and down. **Not only are we wild about God, but God is wild about you! Turn to the people on each side of you and say, "God is wild about you." Call each person by name!** Pause while everyone does this. Then sound the tic tac drum to get everyone's attention.

SAY: I'm [your name], The Mane Event Leader, and I'm here to welcome you to—you'll never guess—The Mane Event! At the end of each day, we'll experience lots of fun-filled activities that help us learn about God and his awesome love for us. Be sure your Safari Crew gets here on time for this celebration.

Today we learned that you and I know God. ("Wow!") Whenever you hear someone say each day's Bible Point, I want you to shout "Wow!" and do the motions. Place your fists by

I know a great idea! Connect with the Sing & Play Roar Leader ahead of time to be sure he or she knows what to do!

"Wow!"

your mouth, then fling your fingers wide open.** Show kids how to do the sign (see photos).

Ask a volunteer to hold the poster of Zach the Zebra, and ask another child to hold the paper torch. **SAY: Today we learned that God helped Gideon and his tiny army to beat the mad, mean Midianites. All Gideon and his tiny army had to use were trumpets and torches inside of jars. But Gideon had our mighty God on his side too.** Ask the volunteer who's holding the torch to wave it.

Gideon knew God! 📖 **I know God!** ("Wow!") 📖 **You know God too!** ("Wow!")

Who can tell me why Zach the Zebra reminds us of today's Bible Point? Look for answers such as "Zach is smart and knows a lot," "Zebras' stripes are like a name tag," "Every zebra's stripe pattern is different," or "Zebras know each other by their stripes."

Bring out your Bible and **SAY: At Sing & Play Roar, you learned today's Treasure Verse from the Bible, Psalm 135:5. The Treasure Verse says, "I know the greatness of the Lord." Say the Treasure Verse with me and do the actions!** Point to yourself on "I," make muscleman arms on "greatness," and raise both arms on "Lord." Ask the kids to repeat the verse along with the actions.

Let's sing "I Want to Know You (In the Secret)" as a prayer to our great God who loved Gideon and who loves us too.

🎵 **TRACK 2** Encourage the volunteers to stay up front and help the Sing & Play Roar Leader lead kids in singing and doing the motions to "I Want to Know You (In the Secret)."

Ask the volunteers to sit down, then **SAY: We learned a lot about Gideon today. At first, Gideon might have been afraid.** Crouch low and ask everyone to crouch low too. **Gideon might have felt really small with only his tiny army to help him beat the mad, mean Midianites.** Stretch tall with your arms held high and ask everyone to do the same. **But Gideon knew God was bigger and mightier than any Midianite army. Gideon knew God would help him be strong!** Ask everyone to sit down.

I KNOW YOU CAN!

SAY: I have an experiment for us to try. But before we do, think of a time you feel afraid like Gideon might have been at first. Maybe there's a bully at your school, or maybe you're afraid of the dark. God helped Gideon defeat the army of Midianites. God helps us, too. I know that God will help us when we're afraid. Let's try an experiment to see what this might look like.

Ask two older boys to come to the front and hold the brooms about twenty inches apart. (Make sure the rope is wrapped back and forth around the broom handles.) Ask a younger volunteer to come up and hold the end of the rope. **SAY: When I say "Go,"** [name of child] **will pull on the rope and try to bring the two broom handles together. The two broom holders will try their hardest to**

HINTS FROM THE HERD

It was only the first day at The Mane Event, and already kids were clamoring to climb onto the stage whenever volunteers were needed! It was a fun problem to have because kids showed so much excitement.

To avoid the commotion on stage, ask another station leader or the Sing & Play Roar Leader to help with volunteer selection during all closing programs. Have the volunteer sit with the crowd and be ready to select kids in the back or on the sides who rarely get picked because they're so far away.

HINTS FROM THE HERD

At our field test, the leader practiced the experiment ahead of time. She asked two adult males to hold the brooms and one little first-grade girl to pull the rope. It worked! The girl had no trouble pulling the rope and bringing the broom holders together.

After The Mane Event, we thought it would have been even more powerful if we had used middle school or teenage boys to hold the brooms. We could have chosen unsuspecting volunteers from the audience. We didn't need to practice it, because it works! The brooms and rope act as a pulley.

keep the brooms apart. **Pretend [name of child] is Gideon and the broom holders are the mad, mean Midianites. Do you think Gideon can pull on this rope strongly enough to pull these two big Midianites together?** Wait for kids to shout and cheer. **Gideon! I *know* you can do it! Don't be afraid! Ready? Go!** Lead everyone in cheering.

Clap for the volunteers and ask them to sit down. **SAY: Gideon knew God, and we know God too.** ("Wow!") **The next time you feel afraid, remember how God helped Gideon. I know that God will help you, too. Take a minute to talk in your crews. Answer this question: What are some things you know about God? For example, "I know God helps me when I'm afraid" or "I know God always loves me." Go ahead and talk in your crews.**

After one minute, sound the tic tac drum and get everyone's attention. **I'll take the microphone around the room and hear some of the things you know about God. After each thing is shared, this side of the room** (motion to one side of the room) **will cheer "I know God, yes I do. I know God, how 'bout you?" Then the other side of the room** (motion to the other side) **will respond, "I know God, yes I do. I know God, how 'bout you?" Then I'll choose someone else to tell a thing he or she knows about God, and we'll cheer again.**

Do this several times, so kids hear lots of things they know about God. As a last cheer, have the entire room clap to the beat as they cheer together, "I know God! I know God!"

SAY: We know so many things about God! We can know more about God by reading the Bible. Hold up your Bible. **The Bible is God's Word, and it tells us all about God and his awesome plans for our lives.**

Let's sing a song to celebrate all we know about God.

Invite the Sing & Play Roar Leader to lead kids in singing "My Jesus, He Loves Me." Join in singing the words and doing the actions.

DAILY CHALLENGE

Thank the Sing & Play Roar Leader, then **SAY: Great singing, everyone! In just a minute, I want you to get out those Daily Challenge sheets from your Serengeti Trek Bible Books. You each chose a Daily Challenge during Watering Hole Snacks today. This is one way you plan to "leave" God's love around after Serengeti Trek today. How will you show others that you know God?** ("Wow!") Share how *you* plan to show others you know God. Your personal involvement in the Daily Challenge will help kids realize that we all can share God's love! **Crew leaders, take out the Daily Challenges and help kids fold them in half like this.** Demonstrate how to fold the slip of paper in half.

Now, crew members, wrap the Daily Challenge around your wrist. Take one of your Serengeti Trek stickers, and use it to hold the ends together. Work with a buddy in your crew to put your Daily Challenge around your wrist.

Play "He's the King" from the *Sing & Play Roar Music* CD while crew members work together to put the Daily Challenges around their wrists.

HINTS FROM THE HERD

Since preschoolers didn't wear their Daily Challenges home, we used this time for preschoolers to exit and make their way back to the Lion Cub Club. They received their Bible Activity Pages and Daily Challenges and were dismissed to their parents. On Day 1, however, it's a good idea for them to stay and learn more about Operation Kid-to-Kid.

HINTS FROM THE HERD

The Daily Challenge became an important part of Serengeti Trek. We heard stories of meaningful, touching ways kids shared God's love with this activity. We also discovered that wearing the Daily Challenge was a super way to ensure that the paper made it home! There were no "strays" left at the end of the day!

OPERATION KID-TO-KID™

SAY: Besides doing our Daily Challenges, I know another way we can show others we 📖 know God. ("Wow!") **This week at Serengeti Trek, we're going on a special mission called Operation Kid-to-Kid. Just like Chadder is on a mission to help needy kids, we're going on a mission too. The kids here in [name of your town] and all over the country will be reaching out to kids in Africa.**

Hold up a sample school supply kit. **During this week at Serengeti Trek, we will be collecting brand-new school supplies to create school supply kits. When you go to school, you have lots of pencils, paper, and erasers to use. But some kids in Africa don't have those things to help them learn. Each Safari Crew will create one school kit to send to a child in Africa. Since lots of children will be getting school kits, it's important that all the kits look exactly alike. That way, children won't feel bad that they didn't get something that someone else did.**

Hold up an Operation Kid-to-Kid handout. **SAY:** Safari Crew Leaders, in just a minute, you'll get these handouts from your Crew Bags and give one to each child. Help your crew members write their names on their handouts. Then work together to decide who will bring which items. Some kids may need to bring more than one item, such as a pencil *and* an eraser.**

Once you've decided what you'll bring, circle the item on your handout. It's important that you take this paper home so you can explain Operation Kid-to-Kid to your parents. When you bring in your items, give them to your Safari Crew Leader. He or she will keep the items in your Crew Bag until Chadder's Adventure Theater, where you'll learn more about Operation Kid-to-Kid and the children we'll help.

🎵 Play "Use Me" while crews sign their names, choose their items, and circle them on the handouts.

Invite the Serengeti Trek Director to choose a Prayer Person to close in prayer. The director can make announcements and dismiss the kids.

TREK TIPS

Although you may think that children in your program can't afford to bring any items, don't make that decision for them. It's important that every child has the opportunity to give.

HINTS FROM THE HERD

Through our field test, we discovered that the eraser, pencil, sharpener, and ruler are the least expensive items. Kids who chose to bring two items could bring two of the "cheapies."

Dear Parent,

Group's **SERENGETI TREK** is partnering with World Vision (an international relief organization) to provide school-supply kits for children in Africa. You and your child can help needy children learn and grow through a small contribution.

Each Safari Crew of about five children is on a special mission. They're putting together a school-supply kit made up of the items pictured on the back of this page. Crew members worked together to choose the mission items each person would donate. The one or two items checked are what your child volunteered to donate.

Each kit must include precisely the same items so that foreign customs officials examining the crates containing thousands of kits will not delay or prevent delivery. For example, the crayons must be 24-count, not 16 or 48. Also, the pencils must be yellow, not multicolored. This will also prevent disappointment on the part of children who otherwise might not receive as much as others. Thanks for remembering that as you purchase the item(s).

Items must be new and in their original packaging. The children receiving these kits seldom get anything new. Leaving items in their original packaging will create more excitement for them as they open their kits. (Product brand doesn't matter. The items pictured are simply examples of what you might send.)

Children must bring all items to their Safari Crew Leaders by the last day of Serengeti Trek. If you are unable to donate the item(s) checked, please circle this paragraph and have your child return this sheet to his or her Crew Leader. Thanks for participating in Operation Kid-to-Kid!

Please have your child bring in the checked item(s).

❑ package of 10 or 12 ballpoint pens

❑ package of 7 or 8 yellow pencils (without designs)

❑ 2 steno pads (6x9)

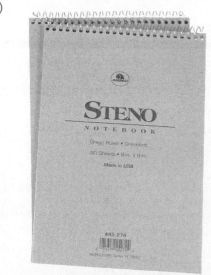

❑ eraser (pink gum type)

❑ pencil sharpener

❑ 24-pack of regular-size crayons

❑ 12-inch ruler with metric markings

BIBLE POINT:
Talk to God.

BIBLE STORY:
Daniel prays and is sent to the den of lions (Daniel 6:1-28).

TREASURE VERSE:
"Pray at all times" (Ephesians 6:18).

THE MANE EVENT
DAY 2

When Nebuchadnezzar conquered Jerusalem, he took many of the young Israelite men into his service. These men—the best and the brightest—would be trained and then be put to use in the king's service. Daniel was one of these young men. During the years of training in Babylon, Daniel lived as a foreigner who was expected to adapt to Babylonian culture, which meant a new name, new foods, and a new religion. But laws and culture couldn't sway Daniel's devotion to God. Faithfully, he prayed. Perhaps Daniel found solace and comfort in his relationship with God. Through prayer, he could stay connected to the God of his people. Even when faced with a den of hungry lions, Daniel refused to stop praying. To Daniel, talking to God was more important than life.

Although society continues to remove prayer from public places, we still have the wonderful freedom to pray. However, the kids at your VBS might still feel a bit like Daniel. They sense the curious stares when they bow their heads to pray in the school cafeteria. They feel like foreigners when they're the only ones not playing a popular video game. That's why prayer is so important in a child's relationship with God. It's a connection to God. It's a reminder of what's really important. It's a place of comfort and acceptance. The activities in today's lesson will help children understand what it means to talk to God.

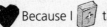 Because I talk to God, I will

- develop a closer friendship with God,

- feel more comfortable talking *about* God,

- have the comfort of an ever-present friend, and

- make choices that honor and please God.

STATION SUPPLIES

For The Mane Event today, you'll need

❏ Bible

❏ CD player

❏ *Sing & Play Roar Music* CD

❏ Bible Point posters and props for Days 1 and 2

❏ Day 2 Daily Challenge (from a Serengeti Trek Bible Book)

❏ game show script (pp. 29-30)

❏ 4 volunteers (3 to be "Daniels" in the game show and 1 to be the "Applause-o-meter")

❏ *Serengeti Trek Skits & Drama* CD

❏ tic tac drum or other attention-getting signal

STATION SETUP

Before kids arrive, photocopy the game show script (pp. 29-30). Rehearse the game show with the three volunteers who are the "Daniels." Show the volunteer who is the "Applause-o-meter" how to record the studio audience's vote for the real Daniel. The Applause-o-meter places one arm on top of the other. He or she raises the top arm according to the loudness level of the applause (see photos).

Place your Bible, posters, and props close by.

ONWARD TO THE EVENT!

SAY: Let's help the rest of the Safari Crews know there's something happening in here! Everyone, give your best Tarzan yell! Lead the kids in shouting "Ah-h-h-h!" Let's sing our theme song while all crews are making their way to The Mane Event!

CD TRACK 1 Lead kids in welcoming the Sing & Play Roar Leader who will lead "He's the King." Join in as everyone sings and does the motions.

"Roarrrr!"

After the song, **SAY: Welcome to Day 2 of The Mane Event—where kids are wild about God.** Ask kids to shout, "We're wild about God!" while they wave their hands overhead and jump up and down.

Ask for volunteers to hold the Zach the Zebra poster and the paper torch. **SAY: Yesterday Zach the Zebra reminded us that you and I...** Encourage the kids to tell you the Bible Point: Know God. You shout "Wow!" Ask a volunteer to hold the Roary the Lion poster. **How do lions talk?** Encourage kids to give their loudest roar. **Lions talk by roaring, and they also talk by moving their tails back and forth. Roary, our friendly lion, helps us remember that we can** **talk to God.** ("Wow!") Choose two volunteers to stand by Roary's poster. Ask them to pretend their arms are the lions' mouths. Have them roar really loud while they open their arms high and low. (See photos.)

In today's Bible story, we learned about Daniel, who refused to stop praying and then was thrown into a den of lions. There weren't just

> Turn the music up nice and loud, so everyone knows a roaring good time is about to begin at The Mane Event!

two lions! **There was a whole** *den* **of lions.** Ask the whole crowd of kids to roar along with the volunteers. **God kept Daniel safe from being lunch for the lions!**

Today's Treasure Verse from the Bible is found in Ephesians 6:18. The Treasure Verse says, "Pray at all times." Clasp both hands together in prayer, then make a circular motion with your hands as if they are hands on a clock going around and around. Encourage kids to repeat the verse and motions with you.

I'm curious...when do you pray? Take the microphone around the group and get several answers. After each answer, have the rest of the group roar like a den of lions. **You guys remember to pray at all times, like Daniel. Don't you worry about a den of lions! God will take care of you.**

Let's sing a song that tells us to pray everywhere and in every way! Invite the Sing & Play Roar Leader to lead "Let Us Pray."

 Encourage the volunteers to stay up front and help lead "Let Us Pray." Afterward, thank the volunteers and the Sing & Play Roar Leader.

WHAT'S MY LION?

SAY: **Daniel prayed to God everywhere and in every way. Even though Daniel knew he would be tossed into a den of lions, he wasn't afraid to pray. Daniel knew it was important to always** 📖 **talk to God.** ("Wow!") **Let's meet the** *real* **Daniel in our game show called** *What's My Lion?*

 Play "Game Show Music" from the *Serengeti Trek Skits & Drama* CD. Clap and cheer as the three contestants enter and take their places up front. Use the following script for the game show.

3 volunteers

Daniel #1: Hi! My name is Daniel.

Daniel #2: Hi! My name is Daniel.

Daniel #3: Hi! My name is Daniel.

Leader: Hi, Daniels. Welcome to our game show *What's My Lion?* I have a few questions for you to answer. Are you ready to begin?

All Daniels: Yes! We're ready!

Leader: OK. Question #1 is, *When* should we pray?

Daniel #1: At least three or four times per day.

Daniel #2: Whenever you feel like it. God knows what we're thinking anyway.

Daniel #3: We need to pray at all times.

Leader: OK. Question #2 is, *How* should we pray?

Daniel #1: Kneeling down is the only way to pray.

Daniel #2: Bowing our heads and folding our hands is the only way to pray.

HINTS FROM THE HERD

Try to get "Daniel" volunteers whom the kids don't know. At the field test, we had the church pastor be the "real" Daniel. When it came time for the kids to vote via the applause-o-meter, we overheard one child say, "It can't be Daniel #3 because his name is Pastor Larry."

HINTS FROM THE HERD

One of the highlights of our VBS field test was listening to the kids pray. Some prayed short, sweet prayers like "Dear God, I love you!" and others prayed longer, more eloquent prayers. Either way, it allowed us to hear just a bit of what God is doing in the hearts of these kids. Don't miss out on this powerful experience! Empower and encourage the kids at your Serengeti Trek to pray.

Daniel #3: There are *lots* of ways to pray. We can kneel, bow our heads, raise our hands, or pray silently. There are *lots* of ways to pray!

Leader: OK! Here's a final question. If there were a law against praying, would you still pray?

Daniel #1: I would still pray, but I'd do it so no one knew I was praying.

Daniel #2: I would pray, but only in the dark and if I was sure nobody could see me.

Daniel #3: I would pray always, even though I knew I'd get in trouble.

Leader: Thank you! OK. Studio audience, it is now time to find out the *real* Daniel. Can I have my Applause-o-meter come forward? *Pause while the volunteer comes forward.* I will point toward the first Daniel. If the studio audience thinks this person is the real Daniel, applaud wildly. The Applause-o-meter will record your response.

Then I will point toward the next Daniel. If the studio audience thinks this person is the real Daniel, applaud wildly. The Applause-o-meter will record your response. Then, we'll do this for the final Daniel. Are you ready?

Do the "applause-o-meter" for each of the Daniels.

Leader: Will the real Daniel please step forward? *All Daniels make fake motions like they are stepping forward, then back. Finally the real Daniel (#3) steps forward. Lead everyone in clapping for him!*

Daniel #3: Remember that we can always 📖 talk to God. *("Wow!")* There are lots of ways to pray...kneeling, standing, sitting, raising hands, you name it! Another way to pray is by singing. Let's pray and sing "Lovely Noise."

CD TRACK 5 Invite the Sing & Play Roar Leader forward to lead "Lovely Noise." Encourage all "Daniels" to stay up front and help lead the singing!

DAILY CHALLENGE™

SAY: In just a minute, I want you to get out those Daily Challenge sheets from your Serengeti Trek Bible Books. You each chose a Daily Challenge during Watering Hole Snacks today. This is one way you plan to "leave" God's love around after Serengeti Trek today. How will you show others that you talk to God? ("Wow!") Share how *you* plan to show others that you talk to God. **Crew leaders, take out the Daily Challenges and help kids fold them in half. Crew members, wrap the Daily Challenge around your wrist. Take one of your Serengeti Trek stickers, and use it to hold the ends together. Work with a buddy in your crew to put your Daily Challenge around your wrist.**

CD TRACK 1 Play "He's the King" from the *Sing & Play Roar Music* CD while crew members work together to put the Daily Challenges around their wrists.

Ask a Prayer Person to say a closing prayer, then have the Serengeti Trek Director make announcements and dismiss the children.

BIBLE POINT:
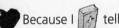 Tell about God.

BIBLE STORY:
Shadrach, Meshach, and Abednego stand up for God (Daniel 3:1-30).

TREASURE VERSE:
"I will tell of all the marvelous things you have done" (Psalm 9:1b).

When King Nebuchadnezzar captured Jerusalem, Daniel's friends Shadrach, Meshach, and Abednego were also taken to Babylon. In Babylon, the three friends served under the most powerful ruler of the time. Nebuchadnezzar considered himself the supreme political and spiritual authority. Dissenting viewpoints or actions were unacceptable and intolerable. So when Shadrach, Meshach, and Abednego refused to bow to Nebuchadnezzar's golden image, the enraged king commanded their gruesome death. The young men didn't know that God would save them. They went to the furnace with the realization that this could be a funeral pyre. Yet amazingly, the three friends stood firm in their love for and belief in the one true God. They boldly proclaimed God's faithfulness. Even when the heat was on, Shadrach, Meshach, and Abednego wouldn't stop talking about God.

Kids today are encouraged to "bow" to many things, from celebrities to bad language. And it's far too easy to fall into bad habits when it seems as if "everyone else is doing it." While younger children are bold in their faith, older kids might feel strange talking about their relationship with God. That's why it's crucial to instill a courageous faith in the hearts of kids today. Help kids discover that they *can* stand up for God—even by simply telling others about him, talking about him, or speaking his name proudly and with reverence. The activities in today's lesson will guide kids as they explore what it means to tell about God.

Because I tell about God, I will

- be bold in sharing my faith,

- let others know more about God,

- show others what it means to be God's friend, and

- help others be bold in their faith.

STATION SUPPLIES

For The Mane Event today, you'll need

❑ Bible

❑ CD player

❑ *Sing & Play Roar Music* CD

❑ Bible Point posters and props from previous days

❑ Day 3 Daily Challenge (from a Serengeti Trek Bible Book)

❑ yellow, orange, and red streamers (enough so each person will have 2 streamers of different colors)

❑ tic tac drum or other attention-getter

STATION SETUP

Before kids arrive, place the streamers by the crew signs so they can be distributed quickly during The Mane Event.

Place your Bible, posters, and props close by.

ONWARD TO THE EVENT!

Play the *Sing & Play Roar Music* CD as Safari Crews arrive from the Serengeti Stations. About one minute before the show is scheduled to begin, tell the kids you want to start a stampede. Lead everyone in clapping their hands and stomping their feet so it sounds like a Serengeti stampede!

After everyone has arrived, **SAY:** Welcome to Day 3 of The Mane Event! It's been another great day at Serengeti Trek, where kids are wild about God! Ask kids to shout, "We're wild about God!" while they wave their hands overhead and jump up and down.

Ask for volunteers to hold the Zach the Zebra poster and the paper torch. **SAY:** On Day 1, Zach the Zebra reminded us that you and I... Encourage kids to tell you the Bible Point: Know God. You shout "Wow!" **Gideon knew God would help him beat the Midianites, and God did!**

Ask a volunteer to hold the Roary the Lion poster. **SAY:** Yesterday Roary, our friendly lion, helped us remember that we can... Encourage the kids to tell you the Bible Point: Talk to God. Ask all the adult leaders to join you in shouting "Wow!" Choose two volunteers to stand by Roary's poster. Ask them to pretend their arms are the lions' mouths. Have them roar really loudly while they open their arms high and low. **Daniel talked to God in his prayers, and God kept Daniel safe from the lions.**

Ask a volunteer to hold the poster of Elaine the Crane. **SAY:** Our chatty buddy Elaine the Crane reminds us to tell about God. ("Wow!") Ask three volunteers to stand next to Elaine the Crane. Give them each a fan to fan their faces, as if they're extremely hot. **Today we learned about three friends—Shadrach, Meshach, and Abednego. Even when the three friends knew they could get thrown into a fiery furnace, they kept telling about God.** ("Wow!")

Hold up your Bible and **SAY:** Today's Treasure Verse is from Psalm 9:1: "I will tell of all the marvelous things you have done." When you say the word "marvelous," make the same motion as when you say "Wow!" Have the kids repeat the verse and actions with you.

Let's sing "Famous One" as if we're singing to the whole world and telling everyone about our awesome God!

Invite the Sing & Play Roar Leader to lead the children in singing "Famous One." Join in singing the words and doing the actions.

> Hello! Let's use our unique voices to tell everyone about God!

Thank the Sing & Play Roar Leader and the volunteers. Help them place the props and posters so everyone can see them. Then **SAY: Today we can face some hot, fiery furnaces of our own. Sometimes we can be like the three friends and stand up for something we know is right, and then we get hurt. Like maybe we go to church and someone teases us for it. Or maybe we stand up for a person who is getting bullied, and the bully starts hurting us. Go ahead and talk in your crews. When is a time you might do what's right, even though you could be hurt? Crew leaders, while crew members talk, hand out the streamers so each person has two streamers of different colors.**

Pause for crews to discuss. Sound the tic tac drum to call attention back to yourself.

SAY: OK! Let's hear about some of those hot, fiery times when you do what's right, even though you could be hurt. The bright streamers you are holding are no longer streamers. They are hot flames in our fiery furnace! Take the microphone around the group. When a child tells you a situation, repeat it so everyone can hear, and **SAY: Ouch! That hurts! If you are holding a yellow flame, shake it high in the air. Our furnace is getting hotter!** Ask another child to tell you a situation, repeat it, and **SAY: Ouch! Ouch! That hurts! If you are holding orange flames, join the yellow flames, and shake them high in the air. Our furnace is getting hotter!** Go to one more child, repeat the situation so all can hear, then **SAY: Ouch! Ouch! Ouch! Our furnace is burning hot! All red flames, join the orange and yellow. Shake the flames high in the air. Look at our hot, fiery furnace. Sometimes it hurts when we do what's right. But doing the right thing is one way we** 🔲 **tell others about God.** ("Wow!") **And just like God helped the three friends, God will help us, too.**

Everyone with a yellow flame, bring it down and shout "Tell!" Ready? "Tell!"

Everyone with an orange flame, bring it down and shout "About!" Ready? "About!"

All those with a red flame, bring it down and shout "God!" Ready? "God!"

Look! The flames are out. We can be bold and brave and do what's right. Doing what's right is one way we 🔲 **tell about God.** ("Wow!") **God helped the three friends, and God will help us, too.**

Have all the kids shake their flames in the air at the same time. Repeat the first fiery situation someone shared. For example: **The next time you see someone who is being picked on...**then have kids lower the flames one color at a time while they shout, "Tell!" "About!" "God!" Ask kids to shake their flames in the air again while you say the next situation. For example: **The next time someone teases you for going to church...**then have kids lower the flames one color at a time while they shout, "Tell!" "About!" "God!" Continue until you've repeated each situation.

Ask kids to shake the flames in the air while you **SAY: The three friends did what was right. They weren't afraid to** 🔲 **tell about God.** ("Wow!") **Even though the three friends were thrown into a fiery furnace, they knew they had to...**then have kids lower the flames one color at a time while they shout, "Tell!" "About!" "God!"

DAILY CHALLENGE™

SAY: In just a minute, we'll do something else that's right! We'll talk about our Daily Challenges. You each chose a Daily Challenge during Watering Hole Snacks. After Serengeti Trek today, how will you show others you 🔲 **tell about God?**

("Wow!") Share how *you* plan to carry out your Daily Challenge today. **Crew leaders, take out the Daily Challenges, and help kids fold them in half. Crew members, wrap the Daily Challenge around your wrist. Take one of your Serengeti Trek stickers, and use it to hold the ends together. Work with a buddy in your crew to put your Daily Challenge around your wrist.**

 Play "Lovely Noise" from the *Sing & Play Roar Music* CD while crew members work together to put the Daily Challenges around their wrists.

Invite the Serengeti Trek Director to make any announcements, then dismiss the kids by Safari Crews in an orderly manner.

BIBLE POINT:
 Love God.

BIBLE STORY:
Jesus dies and rises again (John 19:1–20:18).

TREASURE VERSE:
"We love because God first loved us" (1 John 4:19).

THE MANE EVENT

If anyone had reason to love God wholeheartedly, it was Mary Magdalene. Luke 8:2 says that Jesus freed Mary from the bondage of *seven* demons. She went from living a life of despair to a life of hope and acceptance. Mary understood the power of God, and she also felt the compassion of Christ. She'd experienced Jesus' gentleness, forgiveness, and grace. So when Jesus died on the cross, it's likely that Mary felt her world crashing down around her. Her beloved Jesus was dead. Imagine her astonishment when, three days later in front of an empty tomb, Jesus appeared and lovingly spoke her name.

The word "love" is often overused by kids. "I love ice cream!" "I love playing soccer!" But God's love goes deeper than words can even describe. It's a relationship built from grace and compassion, mixed with forgiveness and devotion. And over all of that, God poured out the blood of his Son, Jesus. Today you have the opportunity to help kids catch a glimpse of that powerful love. Some children may already proclaim a love for God. Use the activities in your lesson to draw children into a deeper, more intimate relationship with God.

Because I love God, I will

- make choices that please God,
- make God a part of my everyday life,
- discover the power of worship, and
- find ways to share God's love with others.

TREK TIPS

Someone will be representing Jesus in a Bible Expedition drama on Day 4. Connect with that person ahead of time to be sure he can stay for The Mane Event.

STATION SETUP

Before kids arrive, ask the person playing Jesus during Bible Expedition to come to The Mane Event. Instruct him to wait outside until all the kids have closed their eyes during the prayer. The actor should carry the white poster board cross and stand in the center of the room. He can exit when you have everyone pray again.

Place your Bible, posters, and props close by.

I *love* experiences like this at Serengeti Trek!

ONWARD TO THE EVENT!

While you're waiting for crews to arrive from the Serengeti Stations, **SAY: While we're waiting for everyone to get here, let's sing some songs! Does anyone have a request?** Lead kids in welcoming the Sing & Play Roar Leader. Join in as everyone sings and does the motions to the songs. Plan to sing the theme song, "He's the King," as the last song of the request time. Hand volunteers the four Bible Point posters and props, and have them help the Sing & Play Roar Leader lead "He's the King."

At the end of the song, have the volunteers stay to help lead another song.

SAY: Wow! Great singing! Welcome to Day 4 of The Mane Event! This has been a great day on Serengeti Trek—where kids are wild about God! Ask kids to shout, "We're wild about God!" while they wave their hands overhead and jump up and down.

Today Gigi the Giraffe reminds us to 📖 **love God.** ("Wow!") **God loves us and gave us his Son, Jesus. Let's sing "To God Be the Glory" as a thank-you to Jesus for dying for us so we could live with him forever.**

🎵 **TRACK 3** Ask the Sing & Play Roar Leader and volunteers to lead kids in singing "To God Be the Glory."

After the song, thank the volunteers for helping. Ask them to set the posters and props so everyone can see them and then return to their seats. **SAY: God loves us so much that he sent his precious Son, Jesus, to die for our sins. Jesus came down from heaven and gave his *life* for us.**

Remember the crew experiment you did at Sing & Play Roar? Let's do it again, only this time we'll say a prayer.

Crew leaders, stand and hold one of your hands up as high as you can. Kids, reach toward your crew leader's hand without letting your feet leave the ground. Pause while crews do this. **Let's pray: Our most high, awesome, powerful God...you are our creator. You made us. You didn't have to come down to us, but you did.**

Crew leaders, now lower your hands and let kids hold your hands. Pause while crews do this. **Let's pray: Thank you, God, for reaching down to us with Jesus' love. We love you. Thank you for loving us first. In Jesus' name, amen.**

Before everyone sits down, have crew members hug people on both sides of them and say,

"God loves you, [person's name]." Then **SAY:** Everyone, give yourself a big hug and say, "God loves me!"

DAY 4

GIVE YOUR LOVE TO GOD

Have everyone sit down. Ask the crew leaders to reach into the Crew Bags and get out the heart stickers. Have them give each crew member a heart sticker to hold.

SAY: Let's pretend these heart stickers represent our love! Hold onto your heart stickers and let's say another prayer. Please bow your heads and close your eyes. While you are praying, have Jesus enter and stand in the center of the group, holding the poster board cross.

Jesus, we love you. Pause. **We want to show our love for you.** Pause. **We want to give ourselves to you so you can use us.** Pause. **In Jesus' name, amen.** Pause.

When you love someone, you will do anything for that person. God loved us so much that he gave us his Son, Jesus. In a moment, you can choose whether you will wear your heart sticker home or give it away to Jesus. It's up to you.

You go first to Jesus and place your heart sticker on the poster board cross. Invite the Sing & Play Roar Leader to sing songs such as "Use Me" (track 9), "More Love, More Power" (track 10), and "Famous One" (track 8). If it feels like nobody is going to give away a heart sticker, you could plan for crew leaders to bring their stickers to Jesus along with you.

When all who wish to give away their heart stickers have done so, **SAY:** **Everyone, please bow your head and close your eyes. Dear Jesus, thank you for reaching down to us and giving us your life. Thank you that we get to live with you forever. We give you our hearts, and we give you our love. In Jesus' name, amen.**

Jesus can exit during the prayer.

SAY: **Jesus loves you so much that he came to be your forever friend. You need to tell Jesus you want to be his forever friend too. If you have more questions about how much Jesus loves you or how to be Jesus' friend, talk with your crew leader or pastor or us! We love because God first loved us. He wants to live with us forever!**

TREK TIPS

If you have more than two hundred participants at your VBS, you could have kids place their heart stickers on their crew signs and sign their names. Then the crew leaders could bring their signs to Jesus.

DAILY CHALLENGE™

SAY: In just a minute, I want you to get out those Daily Challenge sheets from your Serengeti Trek Bible Books. You each chose a Daily Challenge during Watering Hole Snacks. When you leave Serengeti Trek today, how will you show others that you love God? ("Wow!") Share how *you* plan to carry out your Daily Challenge today.

Crew leaders, take out the Daily Challenges, and help kids fold them in half. Crew members, wrap the Daily Challenge around your wrist. Use one of your Serengeti

Trek stickers to hold the ends together. Work with a buddy in your crew to put your **Daily Challenge around your wrist.**

CD TRACK 9 Play "Use Me" from the *Sing & Play Roar Music* CD while crew members work together to put the Daily Challenges around their wrists.

Ask the Serengeti Trek Director to have a Prayer Person pray, then dismiss the kids by Safari Crews in an orderly manner.

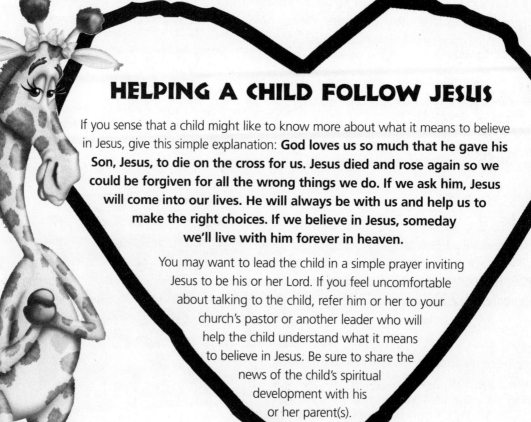

HELPING A CHILD FOLLOW JESUS

If you sense that a child might like to know more about what it means to believe in Jesus, give this simple explanation: **God loves us so much that he gave his Son, Jesus, to die on the cross for us. Jesus died and rose again so we could be forgiven for all the wrong things we do. If we ask him, Jesus will come into our lives. He will always be with us and help us to make the right choices. If we believe in Jesus, someday we'll live with him forever in heaven.**

You may want to lead the child in a simple prayer inviting Jesus to be his or her Lord. If you feel uncomfortable about talking to the child, refer him or her to your church's pastor or another leader who will help the child understand what it means to believe in Jesus. Be sure to share the news of the child's spiritual development with his or her parent(s).

BIBLE POINT:
 Work for God.

BIBLE STORY:
Paul and Silas worship God in prison (Acts 16:16-40).

TREASURE VERSE:
Work hard and cheerfully as though for the Lord (adapted from Colossians 3:23).

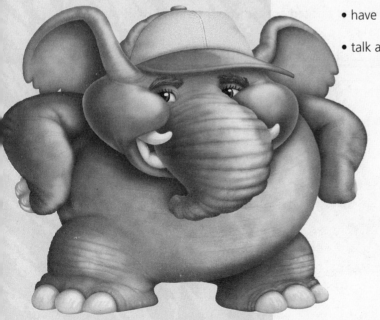

Paul and Silas were not easily discouraged. Imagine being heckled day in and day out by a girl with a persistent evil spirit. Imagine the sense of injustice you'd feel if you were publicly blamed and humiliated for freeing her. Imagine being mobbed by an angry crowd, falsely accused, publicly stripped, severely beaten, and thrown into prison. It's easy to skim over the drastic circumstances of this story simply because we're so familiar with them. What would cause Paul and Silas to think of praising God when their bodies throbbed with pain and every sense was assaulted by their foul surroundings? Simply because they served God. And every action and word was a testimony and an offering to their heavenly Father.

While the kids who attend your VBS probably don't face the intense persecution that Paul and Silas experienced, kids *do* understand what it means to face challenges. It can be hard to get along with siblings every day. It's no fun to congratulate the winners when you're on the losing team. And it's certainly a challenge to give a friend a bigger piece of pizza—or even worse, the very last slice! But each of these difficulties can be put into perspective when we see it as a service to God. Today's activities will help you guide kids to discover the joy that comes when we give God our very best.

 Because I work for God, I will

- do my best in service to God,

- look for opportunities to work for God every day,

- have the courage to do hard things, and

- talk and act like someone who serves God.

STATION SUPPLIES

For The Mane Event today, you'll need

❏ Bible

❏ CD player

❏ *Sing & Play Roar Music* CD

❏ Bible Point posters and props from previous days

❏ Day 5 Daily Challenge (from a Serengeti Trek Bible Book)

❏ tic tac drum or other attention-getter

HINTS FROM THE HERD

We made the Mane Event area look really festive for the last show. After everyone finished snacks, we moved a lot of the decorations from Watering Hole Snacks to The Mane Event. We filled the room with animal-print balloons. It looked "marvelous."

TREK TIPS

Find an empty cargo crate from your decorations. Ask the preschool and Chadder leaders to give you their school supply kits. Place the kits in the crate, and have two strong guys carry it in during The Mane Event.

STATION SETUP

Place the Bible Point posters and props in a line across the front of the room. Ask for volunteers ahead of time to come to the front and hold the posters and props when you ask them to during the event.

ONWARD TO THE EVENT!

While you're waiting for crews to arrive from the Serengeti Stations, ask for song requests. Have the Sing & Play Roar Leader lead the singing.

When everyone has arrived, **SAY:** Welcome to The Mane Event! We've had a great week on Serengeti Trek—where kids are wild about God! Ask kids to shout, "We're wild about God!" while they wave their hands overhead and jump up and down.

Today Lug the Elephant helped us learn that we work for God. ("Wow!") **Give someone nearby a "Lug Hug" and say, "Remember to work for God!"** Pause for everyone to do this.

We've had such a great week at Serengeti Trek. Let's sing "Lovely Noise" as a thank-you to God for giving us such an awesome time together!

Invite the Sing & Play Roar Leader to lead kids in singing "Lovely Noise." Tell the Sing & Play Roar Leader to stay close because you'll need him or her throughout the review.

> Kids know how the attention-getters work by now. So plan to use your tic tac drum to grab kids' attention so you can get started!

WEEK IN REVIEW

SAY: May I have the volunteers I asked earlier stand up here with me? Give Bible Point posters and props to the kids.

On Day 1 at Serengeti Trek, Zach the Zebra taught us to know God. ("Wow!")

"I know   the greatness   of the Lord!"

Gideon knew God would help him beat the Midianites. **Let's hear the Treasure Verse, Psalm 135:5, from the Bible: "I know the greatness of the Lord." Say the Treasure Verse with me and do the actions!** Point to yourself on "I," make muscleman arms on "greatness," and raise both arms on "Lord." Ask kids to repeat the verse along with the actions.

On Day 2 at Serengeti Trek, Roary the Lion re-minded us to  **talk to God.** ("Wow!") **The Trea-sure Verse was Ephesians 6:18, "Pray at all times."** Clasp both hands together in prayer, then make a circular motion with your hands as if they are hands on a clock going around and around. Encourage the kids to repeat the verse and motions with you.

"Pray at all times."

On Day 2, we learned about Daniel, who refused to stop praying and then was thrown into a den of lions. There weren't just two lions! There was a whole *den* of lions. Ask the whole crowd of kids to roar. **God kept Daniel safe from being lunch for the lions!**

On Day 3 at Serengeti Trek, Elaine the Crane reminded us to  **tell about God.** ("Wow!") **God kept the three friends safe in the fiery furnace. They weren't afraid to stand up for God and do what's right. The Treasure Verse was from Psalm 9:1, "I will tell of all the marvelous things you have done." Let's sing a song that tells about our marvelous God.**

CD TRACK 8 Invite the Sing & Play Roar Leader to lead kids in singing "Famous One."

SAY: Yesterday at Serengeti Trek, Gigi the Giraffe reminded us to  love God. ("Wow!") **The Treasure Verse was 1 John 4:19, "We love because God first loved**

HINTS FROM THE HERD

Keep the review moving quickly. By the end of the week, kids were filled with such excitement that they wanted to dance and sing and move!

TREK TIPS

You can vary the way the daily Bible Points and Bible Treasure Verses are presented. Instead of saying all the words, pause before you say a day's Bible Point, and wait for kids to say it. Then you shout "Wow!" (Trust us, they'll be able to say each Bible Point!)

"We love because   God   first

loved   us."

"Work hard and cheerfully
as though for the Lord."

DAY 5

HINTS FROM THE HERD

We played the theme song as kids were exiting. A whole "herd" of kids came to the front to sing "He's the King" one more time! It really looked like a celebration when parents and grandparents picked up their kids.

us." Hug yourself on "We love." Raise arms high on "God," bring them down a bit on "first," then down a bit more on "loved," and hug yourself on "us." Encourage kids to say the words and do the actions with you. **We learned that Jesus died and rose again so we could live forever with him!**

Today at Serengeti Trek, Lug the Elephant reminds us to 📖 work for God. ("Wow!") **Our Treasure Verse from the Bible is from Colossians 3:23. It says to work hard and cheerfully as though for the Lord.** Have kids use their fingers to trace a smile on their faces for "cheerfully," then have them point up for "Lord." Repeat the verse along with the actions.

Ask the kids to hold their hands in front of them as if they are holding on to prison bars. **SAY:** Even though Paul and Silas were put in jail, they cheerfully 📖 worked for God! ("Wow!")

OPERATION KID-TO-KID™

SAY: All week long you've 📖 worked for God. ("Wow!") You've been collecting school supplies to give to needy children in Africa. Good work, Safari Crews! Let's see how many school supply kits we're sending to Africa. While we sing "Must Be Done in Love," my helpers will bring up the kits as an offering to God. Everything we do must be done in love!

🎵 **TRACK 6** Invite the Sing & Play Roar Leader to come up front and lead "Must Be Done in Love." Join in singing the words and doing the actions.

After the song, clap and cheer. **SAY:** Wow! Look at all of these school supply kits. Add up the number of kits you collected. **We're going to spread God's love from here to Africa!**

DAILY CHALLENGE™

SAY: Well, it's time for your final Daily Challenge! But it doesn't *have* to be your final challenge...and it shouldn't be. You can challenge yourself to share God's love every day. When you get home from Serengeti Trek today, how will you show others that you 📖 work for God? ("Wow!")

Share how you plan to carry out your Daily Challenge today. **SAY: Crew leaders, take out the Daily Challenges and help kids fold them in half. Everyone, wrap the Daily Challenge around your wrist and use a Serengeti Trek sticker to hold the ends together. Work with a buddy in your crew to put your Daily Challenge around your wrist.**

Play "Use Me" from the *Sing & Play Roar Music* CD while kids work together to put the Daily Challenges around their wrists.

When crew members have their Daily Challenges on their wrists, thank them for joining you on Serengeti Trek. Remind them once more that God loves them, and invite them to visit your church again soon. Have the director ask a Prayer Person to say a prayer.